Lessons From The Sky

Lessons From The Sky

LJ Ireton

◆ ◆ ◆

ELLIPSIS IMPRINTS

2024

. . .

ELLIPSIS IMPRINTS
Durham, England

. . .

Twitter: @EllipsisImprint

"The Magpie" first appeared in *Minnow Literary Magazine*, May 2021 / "Joining
the Water Birds" first appeared in *Chasing Shadows Literary Magazine*, June
2021 / "The Turtle" first appeared in *Green Ink Poetry*, June 2021 / "Fire Fox
Volta" first appeared in *The Madrigal*, September 2021 / "Queen of the Iris
Stream" first appeared in *Spellbinder Literary Magazine*, October 2022 /
"Lessons from the Sky" first appeared in *Green Ink Poetry*, October 2022 /
"Eco-Psalm" first appeared in *Bud & Branch* by Green Ink Poetry 2022 / "Grey"
first appeared in *The Amphibian Literary Journal*, February 2023 / "Wildflowers,
Waiting" first appeared in *Tiny Seed Journal and Press*, April 2023 / "The
Seahorse" first appeared in *Honeyguide Magazine*, June 2023 / "Reflections
Under a Leaf-Covered Sky" first appeared in *Flint Magazine*, June 2023 / "What
the Sea Told Me" first published Whimsical Press, July 2023 / "Movement in
February" first published by Osmosis Press, October 2023

Lessons From The Sky
Print edition ISBN: 978-1-7397414-5-7
Ebook edition ISBN: 979-8-2155440-6-8

Cover design and internal art by May Glen.

First printing 2024

Contents

Grey

Lines of rain land like soldiers from a plane—
The harsher, heavier side of winter.
When the roads and the sky
Are water-shades of grey,
Daisy desires are lost
Beautiful things in hiding.
The murky wind howls in defence of its place—
The mightiest grey is the wolf,
Fierce in its gaze at you—
Colours roam the earth,
Roaming smoke clouds share canine coats
You are connected to soft things,
Still.

Urban Constellation Under a Polluted Sky

The night shade change is the signal—
Red triangles rise from the tangled, brown
Background line of bushes,
Shape themselves into flame
Russet flickers with white chins.
Their night eyes are imprinted
With the last yellow rings
Of the simmering sun,
Given from one
Fire creature
To another.
Matchstick-tipped paws mark the earth—
Predator patterns, copper-tinged prints,
Light and silent.
Then, the jump—
Ignited across navy horizons
Orange licks across the fur
In the dot-to-dot dance of the fox.
Urban constellation under a polluted sky—
Mud meets mystic feet in humility
Nature's underworld is this
Original fire,
Leaping.
In each flame's luminous heart,
The hottest blue is gentle.
Those who have never seen the sky on earth
Hunt these stars.

Lessons from the Sky

There were six minutes until sunset.
We ran down the sloping road to the beach,
Surprised at others doing the same—
The sun was popular tonight.

It knew. It teased, dipping quickly,
But its parting gift lit up the sea—
A luminescent line highlighting
The poetry remaining in the sky,
Words waiting above the water
For us to read.

Under this beam of light,
An orange sheen hovered wide, and
Curving dark sands framed the water.
From the undulating blue,
Birds flew up and towards us,
Breaking the bright horizon with
Blurry grey wings.

Only then did the poem seem complete—
With the smudges of sea birds night-fishing,
Feathered heartbeats over this thin stretch of yellow.

The strangers didn't speak.
But we all read life between the lines.

The Windmill

The windmill hasn't turned for a hundred years—
Its straight white sails, long still over the fields.
They form a shadow cross on the horizon,
In front of each falling sunset,
Forever marking hidden treasure.

Above the base,
In the criss-cross formation,
Black ink notation lines the staves,
The skeleton—
Each day a murmuration
Of small souls sings out from the mill.
An X-shaped orchestra,
These Starlings are the power,
The product, of this tower now—
Once for grain and corn,
A dark collective of stars
Harvests song.

I imagine the bleached white
And flaking wood arms
Reaching to the sky
Questioning their purpose,
Long ago
To be surprised by a black rain of birds.
I hear their acceptance now,
Their redress.

Winter Lingers Too Long

Winter lingers too long.
Snowflakes dissolved into poems
Months ago,
Yet the steel jaw of sky
Won't give up the Sun.

Spring is in a straightjacket
Somewhere,
Wanting to
Reveal its skin—

The memory of healing
Simmering
Under mine.

Movement in February

The bluetit briefly bows his head
In the shallow end of the dark, melted pond
To drink—
And on leafless trees
The finches flit from pink bud to brown branch,
Hungrily.

The new world has opened
An invisible eggshell fracture
For the small birds—
Letting only them in to taste.
We are still wading through Winter,
Tears of the season on our cheeks,
Watching the birds
For change.

Glimpses of Sun on a Teacup

It is all for
Days like these—
Typing while the tea
Seeps and cools on the side,
Crows with anxiety
Raise cat eyes at the open window
Triangle breeze—
Enough of the world
For now.
Everytime the clouds tease
A divine moment,
White fur rolls towards the
Square of Sun.
There is no obligation
To 'be' any type of person—
Even yourself,
Scattered on the floor
Somewhere with your clothes—
You can pick up the bits you choose
Tomorrow,
Use the same cup
If you want.

The First Springtime Swim

I stretch Winter out under the water
Muscles yawning into light blue—
Blinking away black skies,
Stillness
And who I was on land.

To Convalesce

To convalesce,
I recommend a cat
By your side—
Curled into a crescent moon,
Head upside down and smiling
In her sleep.
Let her show you
The sanctity of stillness
Crafted with circles
And soft shapes.

Queen of the Iris Stream (*Eve i*)

I came across a wild rose bush today—
Brittle in this harsh sun we're not used to, yet.
The outer petals were burnt, dark, dried blood
But inside they were fresh red, a soft, swirled promise.

Nothing burned in The Garden.
Vines dripped with violet sap,
Liquid filled with light flowed over stones, through meadows
To glow in my unstained hands.

I do not know the name of this land,
Dusty and flat beneath our feet
But I know what it is not.
My skin hardens and my hair sways behind my back
As if sweeping the scent of lilac times away as we walk.

But deep down, underneath,
I am still there, queen of the iris stream—
Wet green moss, water lotus at my toes,
Dragonflies fluttering innocent around my head, my soul.

The roses here have two colours,
They know more. Light and dark dance within the same
          flower.

I pick one to take with me into the unknown.

Far From Eden (*Eve ii*)

My feet are dusty.
When I brush the dirt off with my fingers
There are no shallow pools—
Earthen bowls of blue,
Speckled green and white shimmer to clean my hands,
Or give pause to my soul.
The memory of such water swirls around snakes
In my dreams at night.

We shelter in the shade of large stones.
A cat creature lurks nearby—curious,
No longer understanding our language.
Frustration runs through my blood again—
At myself, Adam, at everything,
Even that this new feeling under my skin
Is there at all.

I hear water falling from
Rocks on higher ground
Once there, I find soft green moss
On the bellies of rocks
In the smallest, struggling stream—
I kiss my fingertips in relief
And press them into a tiny damp meadow
No bigger than my palm.
I wonder if it recognises me
So far from Eden.
I recognise life.

I take my wet hands back to land
And press water into the ground in prayer,
I sing a song
Born of The Garden,
Into this place.
There will be roots here,
I tell the staring face of the feline,
Undeterred.

To the Beetle, the Buttercups

To the beetle, the buttercups
Tower, the flowers of the Sun border
The hovering heaven,

The palms of wild flowers
Form sunset hues—
Sky colours swaying on stalks

And dandelion clouds drift over
Grass tips, shape-shifting
With the wind.

We, meanwhile, tread across the earth,
Calling for more nature,
Missing a universe.

Wildflowers, Waiting

We wait, each warming season
Linking arms, an unspoken promise
To surround the young
With wild sweets woven
Pink into the green grass,
A foxglove and violet world
Beyond the water.

This is the nursery that the
Moorhen chicks see—
Meadowsweet soft clouds, lullaby white
To black down wanderings,
Wildflowers the scattered, speckled universe
To eyes just opened
Close to the earth.

Before they learn fear, red coats
And whiskers—all the reasons
To hide,
They will know us—buttercup
Reflections, daisy decorations,
Yellow-dusted purple,
The gentle wild.

As the Pond Grows Colder

Duck weed is gathering green
Forming continents on dark water.
Webbed feet balance on branches
And the moorhen fortifies her twig mound
As the pond grows colder.
A slither of winter
Is snaking the air and under,
The softest warning.
A rat streaks across the stream,
Hurried
And the squirrels have extra handfuls of
Berries
My cardiganed arms are folded—
I too have to store these faces
For when I'm surrounded by walls
And forgetful of the part of me
That lives under trees
And heron wings.

Animal Stories

I am reading myths in the meadow
In the last of the September sun,
When the tree's shadow crawls
Across the clearing
And hovers at my feet.
I rise to go, book closed.
But now is the time
Of the swallow—
I stand still
And water rats and robins appear
So I stay to hear
The animal stories of dusk
Told by the earth itself.

Nature's Rosaries

The Sun pin-points the water—
A floating form of flame

Seaweed lingers on breeze—
Incense made of salt

Dusk-coloured flowers string among the reeds—
Nature's rosaries.

Fire Fox Volta

They are nimble, dainty dancers
Of the dark,
The kings of the galliard—
Lifting and landing,
Paws lightly tapping
The forest floor
In supple, soot-black boots.

Top hats dip to the night
Before tip toe, tip toe
Points,
Bronze bodies bow
Black noses kiss
And flames of fur
Hop in tailored silk coats.

Lithe over leaves
They leap,
Choreographed sparks of
Tail tips
Writing fire letters orange
Into the midnight blue.

Deep in the dawn woods
As ink blue pales,
Their brushed red silhouettes
Remain
Behind branches
And eyelids.

West Wittering

I can see down to the sand
In the shallows of green-tinted water
But as we wade and dip
Meeting the surface light,
It glistens white only,
White, dancing, unsinkable Sun.
Beyond this satisfied, pooled water,
Nesting in gentle cupped sea hands,
A sand bank divides us from the greater expanse,
Blue, full of questions
And distance.
The land, covered at the moon's request,
Is open to us now—
Where waters are parted
We drip and step on to a strip of earth
Beyond time
And walk in-between colour.

Onwards

I was taught that
The clouds are our like our thoughts
They come and go
They thunder, they accuse
They shelter, they surprise
But the sky above them stays the same—
Watches them stir, big and beautiful, frightening—
Aware, but above the stream of movement.
So our minds must be.

My mind can be a catastrophe, often.
But occasionally I catch a glimpse
Of the grey clouds sailing
Whether they like it or not
They float, like the pretty ones,
Onwards.

Rainbow Sometimes

I do not want to see a rainbow sometimes—
I want one, always, in my hands;
To carry mystery-coloured flame through
The smokey street of tired people.

Some will say: 'I want that.'
Others will find it 'distracting.'
Those who favour grey will complain that it's not
'Appropriate.'

And while they argue,
I will stroke the original ghosts
Of colour,
Untouched by fumes or opinion
And keep walking.

Holding the Earth

The Sun has fallen a little,
But stalls on my face
And ponders the daisies,
Ever happy
At my feet.
I press my palms to the earth—
I want to feel this peace
As a tangible thing—
Something I can still hold
When twilight and worry
Wade through the trees.

Harvest

My sunflowers had faded—
Nodding their heads
Like they were ok with it
But I wasn't—
It was disappointing to see them
Depleted of a power
The Sun herself gets to keep
All year round.
I left them for days
Resembling old scarecrows
On their straightening sticks,
Waiting for the harvest.

I brushed my
Fingers over their furry faces
And the black shells underneath leapt into my palms
Like jumping beans.
Earth-dark, plentiful on my pale skin,
Given to me was an interaction
The live flowers couldn't achieve—
An intimate touch, a gathering.

I watched the smiling sunflowers all summer,
Now I realise that beauty has fallen into my hands—
Harvest is holding
And I am the custodian.

The future flowers are watching, waiting on me.

Seeding

I sink my skin into the soil
Place a beginning
Under a black, damp blanket.
I am an instrument
Of the making magic—
The Sun says so.

I touch more places,
But some only see dirt—
Ask me to clean it up.

I can not understand resistance
To scattered bits of beauty.

I have faced it all my life.

What kind of soul
Would not want
This earth

Filled with flowers?

The Creeping Thistle

The creeping thistle has changed
The purple has been replaced
By feather duster heads
That used to be flowers
Soft fur that is able to brush away
Tears
For those who mourn the colour.

Seeds

The gardener, sowing seeds all day
Doesn't expect to see trees by nightfall.

Yet I fold my arms daily
In frustration, waiting.

The Curve

I forget, when stones
Block my way,
That when water flows
Over rocks,
The curve
Catches more light.

Meeting the Moon on the Dirt Path

It is late in the day.
With my feet in the dirt against an old wooden gate,
I watch a faint pink sky meet a darkening blue,
And I wait.

Behind me is the city road.
But on the field ahead, well-trodden grass patched with hay,
A white horse walks—
A muscled moon,
Shaking out the day from his mane
Nudging the evening forward.

His face is chiselled from ancient stone,
Finished with charcoal smudges—
Quick, precise, down the sides
Of his snorting nose.
Elven ears turn to distant city noises
And my own exhaled breath—
His tail flicking high and falling feathered
Stark and light against
The purpling sky and tree bark silhouettes.

I have seen this horse in medieval oils—
This shape is immortal,
Transforming the horizon—
A rival to the Sun itself
Commanding the eye,
Infusing the mind with a glimpse of mystic
In one turn of his head.

Around me, the metals of the city
Melt—
I lean on a gate
To somewhere else.

Floating Dinner Plates

I watched a water rat
Eat out of curled up leaves
At the bank of a stream.
They were drifting
Like paper boats
At the end of a race,
But the little rat
Pulled each one close
And peered inside eagerly to see
What it held.
We look for magic everywhere,
While every day
Nature transforms
Dried, fallen leaves
Into floating dinner plates,
Herself.

Eco-Psalm

The earth was black—
Nothing but a surface soil of dark
Isn't that how all stories start?
Because life is growing underneath
The dirt, the dust—
The struggle, the magic
The first sprouting or the fight back up.
What is sudden, was sown once—
Tiny, pushing, pale green leaves release
Forests of hope
In the moment you see them.
Because colours will come,
Wild red embers from the Sun,
Burning flame flowers across
Once barren fields
Like you've never seen.
And yet recognise— As if they have grown
On the surface of your heart
Because we have always known
That seeds are meant to fall apart
Before they become,
But we forget
Until we are in the bloom.

The Magpie

The rain had sunk into the pavement,
Dark grey and shining silver
Under a watchful magpie's eye.
The Sun was relieved
It could finally soothe
The landscape after the storm—
It projected a rose gold hue
Over all the white houses in response.
Ever the entrepreneur,
The wily magpie now flew
Directly through the Sun's setting fire,
Colouring his white feathers pink
And blushing
Under his sleek black wings.
I have seen magpies
Take many things—
But a shade of sunset
Is a select achievement.

Joining the Water Birds

I wait
To grace the wild waters
Where geese glide under trees
And small fish hide from shadows.
I imagine the Sun
Redeeming my cold limbs
As I swim without any ceiling
Feeling the air and light and liquid
The way other creatures know them.
I want to learn the history of the earth
By joining the water birds
In the place where buildings
Were never made—
Where mirrors are as
Soft as the sky.

What the Sea Told Me

I speak to the sea each falling night,
Hovering on the wet sand.
She reveals relics, sharp ceramics
Soft salt seaweed
And other things to stir—
Soaked sticks and plastic skins
Chipped shells—some shimmering underneath
And fresh memory of humans and fish—

I mix them in,
Sifting the song and scent
Of the sun hours
Spent underwater
To lift
As she retreats.

Then I scatter
Hope and decay—
The day invisible
Across the shoreline.

In the dark,
Feet on land, face to sky
You breath it in,
Slowly
With no words—
What the sea told me.

The Ambitious Dormouse

They said it couldn't be done
That no-one touches the Sun—
But he was a good climber,
Tail curled for this purpose,
With whiskers ready to twitch for any dangers.
So he rose above their words—
One by one each tiny claw scaled
The thick, tall, stalk
Striped and towering
Over the fellow yellow fields.

He knows that the earth holds the sky
That this is his world—
A hovering sun in the night hours.
His nose nudges the centre
Of the sunflower,
And two brown circles, both risen from the ground,
Combine, swaying slightly.
He rests at height as dawn climbs after him,
Smiling as he closes his eyes.

The Turtle

The abandoned pond
Is not far from the roads,
But the rings of thick mud
Keep the humans away.
The surrounding overgrown trees
Have a pact to protect
This place,
So the magpies wash
And the ducks dip
Safe in sanctuary.
I have always come here,
But today I am stunned—
On a sideways tree trunk
That slopes into the water
Is the unmistakable shape of a shell.
It is so rare to find a turtle
Here in this city,
But there is his head—
Out and up
Being anointed by the Sun.
He looks like an ancient king,
A myth from the murky place
Who has crawled out
Into a forgotten, urban corner
And likes it that way.

The Seahorse

Dragons exist.
The chimera kind—
Black horse is
Fused dragon is
Pastel pink fish.

All creatures is he—
Bones and fin,
Fire-shape without
The flame
A crowned yellow silver
And maneless green
Spiked curve of the
Underworld.

His tail holds on to reality,
Straight lines of grass
Rooted in the sea bed
To keep him
From floating into myth,
Beside Poseidon.

Reflections Under a Leaf-Covered Sky

The weight of fault, disorder
Behind my eyes
I take to what most resembles Eden—
I find I can't cry
Until I am under a leaf-covered sky,
The realm of feather song
Where only blossom falls
And the peopled, stone world
Seems sunken under this one.

At the stream I see a moorhen,
Stood on a mound of mud brown,
Very still—
He, too has mystery on his mind.
Minutes later, he tests the water
With each foot before going back in.
I think of the human proverb:
There is a time to weep.
I watch the bird answer:
And a time to swim.

The White Searching

I took my soul closer
To the beginning
Mingling with another,
Another green
This early evening
But the squirrels were sleeping,
The small birds too high.
I sat at the overflowing
Of the stream
Cow Parsley in front of the fall
Delicate enough to
Meditate on—
Until the turn of my head
Caught an egret
White above the water
Stepping through
The slow seconds
I tried to hold still.
Finally a reminder
Of the other lived world
The fishing and foraging one
With angel feathers—
This was why I had come
To be where creatures seek
And not pull down others,
To search
And join in the searching.

Blossoms to Black

The river was low,
Remaining water lined
With brown blossom days old.

The crow landed—
A carved coal figure
On moving light patches,
Beak in the petals.

When I approached,
The wind rose, nudging the trees,
The forest threw its bouquet from canopy arms
And blossom rained down
Rose drops, yellowing blurs
Over the black bird.

He raised his head into the fairy-like falling—
Wisdom-seeking.
A portrait of ancient omen
From the bank—
Some think death,
Others transformation.

I saw a scavenger of beautiful moments
Or perhaps I am one—
Pink rain is prettiest against
The darkest wing.

Stone Shadows

At the deepest part of the stream,
Young silver-green fish dart
Into the dark parts
Of piled-up rocks—
A rubble edge of a new world.

Their white fins flap in the finding—
Sunken stones are waiting shadows,
A shelter for tiny slippery souls.

But their side eyes re-emerge
Looking older.
In the sleek space of black,
A pause in the dip and rise—
Safety has changed colour.

They are cautious leaving these
Stone shadows now.
Minute lights flicker on and off
Under the water—
Decisions in small silk bodies.

On the Wild Water

The lake bites, pre-historic,
Cold—
When clouds come
Black ink spreads under my limbs.

I swim into wet green sun—
Less unknown,
And towards a lone white beak.

Here I hover, held by red eyes—
Electric on the wild water
Deciding
On the natural
In me.

About the Poet

LJ is a vegan poet and a bookseller from London. She has a 1st Class B.A. Honours in English Language and Literature from the University of Liverpool. Her poems have been published by numerous journals both in print and online, including, *Minnow Literary*, *Green Ink Poetry*, *The Madrigal*, *Noctivagant Press*, *Spellbinder Literary Magazine*, *Drawn to the Light*, *Acropolis Journal*, *Mausoleum Press*, *Cerasus Magazine*, *Amphibian Literary Journal*, *Tiny Seed Journal*, and *Flint Magazine*.

Her poetry features in the printed anthology *Spectrum: Poetry Celebrating Identity* by Renard Press (2022) and the *York Literary Review 2023* by Valley Press.

Also available from
Ellipsis Imprints

✦ ✦ ✦

❧   *Conjunction* by S.M. Rosen
      Fresh, accesible, and bursting with poignant allusions, Rosen's
poems speak to any heart that has loved, lost, and sought meaning
in a world that seems both altogether too big and too small.

❧   *Songs for Winter Rain* by Sophie Grace Chappell
      In this debut poetry collection, Chappell examines faith and
interrogates it. Her language is rich, revealing, involveing both the
heart and head of the reader, and evoking a longing to leave the
built-up south for a world of more intimate understanding.

❧   *Striking Bodies, Striking Minds* edited by Sara L. Uckelman
      Stories, poetry, songs, art, and more from the 2018, 2019, and
2020 higher education strikes in the United Kingdom. Proceeds
from the sale of this charity anthology are donated to the Universi-
ties and Colleges Union Fighting Fund.

For more information, go to
https://ellipsisimprints.com/
or visit us on X/Twitter: @EllipsisImprint

Milton Keynes UK
Ingram Content Group UK Ltd.
UKHW051317110624
444061UK00040B/561